Simple Grill Cookbook for Beginners

Incredibly Delicious Grill Recipes for The Electric Grill

BY: GRACE BERRY

www.graceberry.net

License Notes

This book is an informational material. The author has taken great care to ensure the correctness of the content. However, the reader assumes all responsibility of how the information is used, and the author shall not be accountable for any form of misuse or misinterpretation on the part of the reader.

Table of Contents

Introduction

Congrats on owning your personal grill! Now, you will be able to create and prepare some delicious smoked meals from the comfort of your backyard. Before attempting to light your new tool and indulge in cooking, you must be made aware of some fundamental things. Now, let's get you familiarized with your grill and the necessary tools needed for success.

It is very important to season your grill before you start cooking. These instructions are usually found in the manual, which accompanied the grill, read carefully. If you have ever seasoned an iron pan, seasoning the grill is very similar.

Simply coat the inside with some oil readily available in your pantry, even a little bacon grease can do the trick. Once the entire grill surface is coated with oil, go ahead and heat it. Heating will ensure the oil is spread evenly throughout. The oil Coating act as protection against various natural elements.

Ensure the heat is gauged between 250-275 degrees F. Anything higher will remove the paint. The oil will prevent rust on the grill.

Come now, let's enjoy these recipes!

Kale Sausage Breakfast

This breakfast is simple yet delicious.

Serves: 4

Time: 20 mins.

Ingredients:

- onion (1 medium, yellow, sweet)
- eggs (4 medium)
- sausage (4, links)
- kale (2 cups, chopped)
- mushrooms (1 cup)
- Olive oil (as required)

Directions:

1. Firstly, arrange your Electric grill over kitchen platform then open the top lid.

2. Next, arrange the grill grate then close top lid. Press the "GRILL" function then select "HIGH" grill function.

3. Adjust timer to approximately 5 minutes then press "START/STOP." Your electric grill will start to pre-heat.

4. Once your electric grill is fully functional and preheated it should beep. Once you hear a beep, open the top lid. Arrange sausages evenly over grill grate.

5. Close top lid then, cook for approximately 2 minutes and open the top lid. When finished flip the sausages.

6. Close top lid then, cook for an additional 3 minutes.

7. Remove the grilled sausages then lightly grease a multi-purpose using some cooking oil and spread the mushrooms, onion, and kale.

8. Add the sausages (grilled) then crack the eggs in between sausages. Open lid then arrange pan directly inside pot.

9. Press "BAKE" then adjust temperature to 350 degrees F. Adjust timer for 5 minutes then press "START/STOP."

10. Close top lid then allow to cook until timer reads zero. Serve warm.

Classic Cinnamon Almond Oats

For a simple oatmeal try out this recipe.

Serves: 4

Time: 25 mins.

Ingredients:

- Almonds (½ cup, slivered, blanched)
- Butter (2 tablespoons, unsalted)
- Oats (1 cup, Steel-cut)
- Vanilla extract (½ teaspoon)
- Cinnamon (¼ teaspoon ground)
- Kosher salt (¼ teaspoon)
- Sugar (2 tablespoons)
- Water (2 cups)
- Whole milk (1 cup)

Directions:

1. Place the Electric grill multi-cooker over a cooking platform, then open the top lid.

2. Place a reversible rack and place the Crisping Basket over the rack into the pot. In the basket, add the almonds.

3. Close the multi-cooker using the crisping lid; make sure to keep the pressure release valve locked/closed.

4. Select the "AIR CRISP" setting and adjust the 375°F temperature level.

5. Afterwards, set timer to 5 minutes and press "STOP/START"; this will start the cooking process by storing up the pressure inside.

6. When the timer finishes, quickly release pressure by changing the pressure valve to the VENT.

7. After pressure releases, remove the pressure lid. Set aside the almonds and take out the basket and rack.

8. In the pot, add the butter; Select "SEAR/SAUTÉ" mode and select "MD: HI" pressure level.

9. Press "STOP/START." After about 4-5 minutes, the butter will start simmering.

10. Add the oats and cook (while stirring) for about 2-3 minutes until they become softened. Mix in the Add the salt, sugar, vanilla, cinnamon, water, and milk.

11. Seal the multi-cooker by locking it with pressure lid then ensure to keep pressure release valve locked or sealed.

12. Select "PRESSURE" mode and select the "HI" pressure level. Then, set timer to 10 minutes and press "STOP/START"; it will start the cooking process by building up inside pressure.

13. When the timer goes off, naturally release inside pressure for about 8-10 minutes. Then, quick release pressure by adjusting the pressure valve to the VENT.

14. After pressure gets released, open the pressure lid. Serve warm using almonds (toasted) on top then enjoy!

Coconut Breakfast Bagels

These Coconut Breakfast Bagels are a great way to start any day.

Serves: 4

Time: 18 mins.

Ingredients:

- sugar (1 cup, fine)
- black coffee (2 tablespoons, prepared and cooled down)
- bagels (4, halved)
- coconut milk (1/4 cup)
- coconut flakes (2 tablespoons)

Directions:

1. Arrange Electric grill over your kitchen platform, then open the top lid. Arrange grill grate evenly then close top lid.

2. Press the "GRILL" function then select "MED" grill. Adjust timer to 4 minutes then press "START/STOP."

3. Electric grill should begin pre-heating. Once Electric grill is preheated and full functional it should start beeping.

4. Once you hear a beep proceed to open the top lid. Arrange 2 bagels evenly over grill grate.

5. Close top lid then cook for approximately 2 minutes. Now open top lid then, start flipping the bagels.

6. Stop lid then cook for an additional 2 minutes.

7. Allow cooking until timer reads zero then divide among serving plates.

8. Grill remaining bagels in a similar way then whisk the remaining ingredients in a mixing bowl.

9. Serve the bagels (grilled) with the freshly prepared sauce on top.

Pineapple French Toast

This mix shouldn't work, but it so does.

Serves: 4-5

Time: 25 mins.

Ingredients:

- Bread (10 slices)
- sugar (¼ cup)
- Milk (1/4 cup)
- Eggs (3, large)
- Coconut milk (1 cup)
- Pineapple (10 slices, 1/4-inch-thick, peeled)
- Coconut flakes (1/2 cup)
- Cooking spray

Directions:

1. Using a mixing bowl, whisk the sugar, coconut milk, eggs and milk. Dip the bread in the mixture and leave for about 2 minutes.

2. Place the Electric grill over your kitchen platform and open the top lid. Set up the grill grate and close the top lid.

3. Press "GRILL" and select the "MED" grill setting. Adjust the timer to 4 minutes and then press "START/STOP." Electric grill will begin pre-heating.

4. When the Electric grill starts to beep it is preheated and ready to cook. Once you hear a beep, begin to open top lid.

5. Place half the bread slices over the grill grate.

6. Close lid then cook for approximately 2 minutes. Now open the top lid and flip the slices.

7. Close the top lid and cook for 2 more minutes.

8. Allow cooking until the timer reads zero. Divide into serving plates.

9. Repeat with the remaining slices. And then grill the pineapple slices with the same amount of time (flipping after 2 minutes).

10. Serve warm with the grilled bread topped with some coconut flakes.

Egg Broccoli Quiche

This delicious quiche can be whipped up in minutes and can serve the whole family.

Serves: 6

Time: 30 mins.

Ingredients:

- Eggs (8, medium)
- Milk (½ cup)
- Cheddar cheese (1 cup, shredded)
- Olive oil (1 tablespoon, extra-virgin)
- sea salt (1 teaspoon)
- black pepper (1 teaspoon ground)
- garlic cloves (2, minced)
- onion (1 yellow, chopped)
- broccoli florets (2 cups, thinly sliced)
- piecrust (1, at room temperature)

Directions:

1. Whisk the 8 eggs then add gradually add in the salt, milk, and pepper into a mixing bowl.

2. Next, add the cheddar cheese then whisk well.

3. Arrange your Electric grill multi-cooker, over a cooking platform, then open top lid.

4. Add the oil into the pot then select the "SEAR/SAUTÉ" mode then select the "HIGH" pressure level.

5. When finished press the "STOP/START." After about 5 minutes, oil should start simmering.

6. Add the garlic and onions then cook (while occasionally stirring) for approximately 5 minutes until it becomes softened and translucent.

7. Add broccoli then sauté for an additional 5 minutes.

8. Add over the egg mixture then gently stir-cook for approximately 1 minute until eggs are thoroughly cooked incorporate.

9. Add the mixture into the pie crust then fold edges. Make a small cut into the center of the piecrust for heat escape.

10. Seal multi-cooker by using crisping lid to lock it; ensure to keep pressure release valve locked/sealed.

11. Select "BROIL" mode then select the "HIGH" pressure level. Then, set timer to approximately 10 minutes then press "STOP/START"; it should start the cooking process by building up inside pressure.

12. When the timer has expired, then, quick release pressure by adjusting the pressure valve to the VENT.

13. After pressure has released, open pressure lid. Slice and serve pie warm and enjoy!

Bacon Tomato Omelet

Family breakfast can be fun again with this recipe.

Serves: 4

Time: 20 mins.

Ingredients:

- Eggs (4, whisked)
- Cheddar (1 tbsp., grated)
- Bacon (¼ pound, cooked and chopped)
- Tomatoes (4, cubed)
- Parsley (1 tbsp., chopped)
- Olive oil (1 tbsp.)
- Black pepper (ground, salt to taste)

Directions:

1. Place the Electric grill multi-cooker over a cooking platform, then open the top lid.

2. Pour the oil into the point, Select "SEAR/SAUTÉ" mode and select "MD: HI" pressure level. Press "STOP/START." After about 4-5 minutes, the oil will start simmering.

3. Add the bacon and cook (while stirring) until it becomes crisp for 2 minutes.

4. Add all the other ingredients excluding the cheese and whisk the mixture. Add the cheese on top.

5. Seal multi-cooker by using crisping lid to lock it; ensure to keep pressure release valve locked/sealed.

6. Select "BAKE/ROAST" mode and adjust the 400°F temperature level. Then after, set timer to 8 minutes and press "STOP/START," it will start the cooking process by building up inside pressure.

7. When the timer goes off, quickly release pressure by adjusting the pressure valve to the VENT. After pressure gets released, open the Crisping Lid. Serve warm.

Sausage Corn Frittata

This frittata will be a hit with the whole family.

Serves: 4

Time: 30 mins.

Ingredients:

- Corn (½ cup)
- Sausage (1 chorizo, diced)
- Eggs (1 chorizo)
- Milk (1 cup)
- Potato (1, diced)
- Feta cheese (8 oz., crumbled)
- Sea salt
- Black pepper (ground)
- Water (1 cup)

Directions:

1. Using a mixing bowl, whisk the eggs and the milk thoroughly. Season using salt and black pepper.

2. Grease a baking pan using cooking spray, vegetable oil, or butter. Add and mix the corn, potato and chorizo.

3. Pour the egg mixture and feta cheese in. Place the Electric grill multi-cooker on to a cooking platform, then open the top lid.

4. Place a reversible rack and put the pan on top.

8. Close multi-cooker by using crisping lid to lock it; ensure to keep pressure release valve locked/sealed.

5. Select "PRESSURE" setting then select the "HI" pressure level. Afterwards, set the timer to approximately 20 minutes and press "STOP/START," this will start the cooking process by building up pressure inside.

6. When the timer goes off, quickly release pressure by changing the pressure valve to the VENT. Afterwards, open the pressure lid. Serve warm.

Potato Chips

This potato chips are healthy, crisp, and delicious.

Serves: 2-3

Time: 8 -10 hrs. 10 mins.

Ingredients:

- Potato (1 sweet, peeled and cut into slices)
- sea salt (½ teaspoon)
- avocado oil (½ tablespoon)

Directions:

1. Toss the slice and avocado oil, into a mixing bowl until evenly coated. Season using salt to taste.

2. Place the Electric grill multi-cooker over a cooking platform, then open the top lid.

3. Evenly arrange Crisping Basket inside the pot. Press "DEHYDRATE" then adjust temperature to 120 degrees F.

4. Adjust the timer to approximately 8 hours then press "START/STOP." Electric grill should start to pre-heat.

5. Once Electric grill starts to beep it is preheated and ready to cook. After a beep has occurred, open the top lid.

6. Arrange slices into a single layer directly inside basket. Close top lid then, allow to cook until timer reads zero.

7. Dehydrate for an additional 2 more hours if slices are not crisp enough. Serve warm.

Appetizing Peppers

These grill peppers are delicious with a tomato sauce dip or stuffed with minced beef.

Serves: 4

Time: 22 mins.

Ingredients:

- tomato sauce (2 ounces)
- onion (1 green, chopped)
- bell pepper (1 orange, cut into strips)
- bell pepper (1 yellow, cut into strips)
- oregano (2 tablespoons, chopped)
- Black pepper (ground) and salt to taste

Directions:

1. Place the Electric grill multi-cooker over a cooking platform, then open the top lid.

2. Add the ingredients in the pot, then stir gently. Seal multi-cooker by using the pressure lid to lock.

3. Select the "PRESSURE" mode then select the "HIGH" pressure level.

4. Set timer to approximately 12 minutes then press "STOP/START," it should start the cooking process by building up inside pressure.

5. Once the timer goes off, quickly release pressure by adjusting the pressure valve to the VENT.

6. After pressure gets released, open the pressure lid. Serve warm.

Mayonnaise Corn

Serve this tasty corn as a snack or a side dish.

Serves: 3-4

Time: 24 mins.

Ingredients:

- Sour cream (¼ cup)
- Mayonnaise (¼ cup)
- Corn (3 ears, husked, rinsed and dried)
- Olive oil spray
- Garlic powder (½ tsp.)
- Chili powder (¼ tsp.)
- cotija cheese (¼ cup, crumbled)
- Lime juice (¼ cup, crumbled)
- Cilantro leaves (Fresh, for garnish)
- Salt (½ teaspoon)
- Black pepper (½ tsp., ground)

Directions:

1. Place over a cooking platform and open the top lid.

2. In the pot, place the Crisping Basket and coat with some cooking spray. In the basket, add the corn.

3. Seal multi-cooker by using crisping lid to lock it; ensure to keep pressure release valve locked/sealed.

4. Select "AIR CRISP" mode and then adjust the 400°F temperature level. Then after, set timer to 12 minutes and press "STOP/START," it will start the cooking process by building up inside pressure. Shake the basket after 6 minutes.

5. When the timer goes off, quickly release pressure by adjusting the pressure valve to the VENT.

6. After pressure gets released, open the Crisping Lid. Add the corn on a plate.

7. Stir together the mayonnaise, sour cream, lime juice, cheese, garlic powder, and chili powder into a mixing bowl. Add the cream mixture over the corn.

8. Use salt and black pepper to season to taste. Top using cilantro, and more chili powder.

Blooming Onion Crisps

Here, we have a snack even the kids can enjoy.

Serves: 4-6

Time: 30 mins.

Ingredients:

- eggs (2 medium)
- onion (1 large, sliced)
- milk (2 tablespoons whole)
- powder (1 teaspoon garlic)
- paprika (1 teaspoon)
- breadcrumbs (1 cup panko)
- Olive oil (to taste)

Directions:

1. Beat the eggs then add the milk into a mixing bowl and stir to combine.

2. In another bowl, combine the seasoning and breadcrumbs. Add the onions; coat well and tip over; remove excess drip.

3. Take Electric grill multi-cooker, arrange it over a cooking platform, and open the top lid.

4. In the pot, arrange a reversible rack and place the Crisping Basket over the rack. In the basket, add the onion mixture.

5. Seal multi-cooker by using crisping lid to lock it; ensure to keep pressure release valve locked/sealed.

6. Select the "AIR CRISP" mode and adjust the 390°F temperature level. Then, set timer to 10 minutes and press "STOP/START"; it will start the cooking process by building up inside pressure.

7. If not crispy, continue cooking for 4-5 more minutes. When the timer goes off, quick release pressure by adjusting the pressure valve to the VENT.

8. After pressure gets released, open the pressure lid. Serve warm and enjoy!

Creamed Potatoes

Grilled potatoes can be creamy too. Give this recipe a go.

Serves: 4

Time: 30 mins.

Ingredients:

- canola oil (1 tablespoon)
- Black pepper (finely ground, and salt to the taste)
- Potatoes (2 gold, cut into wedges)
- heavy cream (3 tablespoons)

Directions:

1. Take Electric grill multi-cooker, arrange it over a cooking platform, and open the top lid.

2. In the pot, arrange a reversible rack and place the Crisping Basket over the rack. In the basket, add the potatoes.

3. Seal multi-cooker by using crisping lid to lock it; ensure to keep pressure release valve locked/sealed.

4. Select the "AIR CRISP" mode and adjust the 400°F temperature level.

5. Then, set timer to 10 minutes and press "STOP/START"; it will start the cooking process by building up inside pressure.

6. When the timer goes off, quickly release pressure by adjusting the pressure valve to the VENT. After pressure gets released, open the lid. Set aside the potatoes and set aside the Crisping Lid.

7. In the main pot, add the oil; Select "SEAR/SAUTÉ" mode and select "MD: HI" pressure level.

8. Press "STOP/START." After about 4-5 minutes, the oil will start simmering.

9. Add the potato wedges, salt, pepper, and heavy cream and cook (while stirring) until they become softened for 8-10 minutes. Serve warm.

Cauliflower Soy Carrots

This delicious meal makes for a super filling dinner.

Serves: 4

Time: 20 mins.

Ingredients:

- peas (½ cup)
- carrot (1, cubed)
- onions (2 spring, chopped)
- cauliflower (3 cups, florets separated)
- garlic cloves (2, minced)
- olive oil (2 tablespoons)
- soy sauce (2 ½ tablespoon)
- A pinch of black pepper (finely ground) and salt

Directions:

1. Take Electric grill multi-cooker, arrange it over a cooking platform, and open the top lid.

2. In the pot, add the oil; Select "SEAR/SAUTÉ" mode and select "MD: HI" pressure level.

3. Press "STOP/START." After about 4-5 minutes, the oil will start simmering.

4. Add the onions, garlic, and cook (while stirring) until they become softened and translucent for 2-3 minutes.

5. Add the carrots, cauliflower, soy sauce, salt, black pepper, and peas; stir the mixture.

6. Seal multi-cooker by using crisping lid to lock it; ensure to keep pressure release valve locked/sealed.

7. Select "PRESSURE" mode and select the "HI" pressure level. Then, set timer to 8 minutes and press "STOP/START"; it will start the cooking process by building up inside pressure.

8. When the timer goes off, naturally release inside pressure for about 8-10 minutes.

9. Then, quick-release pressure by adjusting the pressure valve to the VENT. Serve warm.

Mayonnaise Carrots

These grilled carrots are coated in a thin layer of mayonnaise to make a delicious side.

Serves: 4

Time: 16 mins.

Ingredients:

- horseradish (2 tablespoons grated)
- mayonnaise (¾ cup
- carrots (1 pound, peeled and cut into 1-inch pieces)
- vegetable stock (½ cup)
- kosher salt (½ teaspoon)
- black pepper (½ teaspoon ground)
- Minced parsley

Directions:

1. In mixing bowl, add the horseradish, mayonnaise, salt, and pepper. Combine the ingredients to mix them well with each other.

2. Take Electric grill multi-cooker, arrange it over a cooking platform, and open the top lid. In the pot, add the stock and carrots.

3. Seal multi-cooker by using crisping lid to lock it; ensure to keep pressure release valve locked/sealed.

4. Next, select "PRESSURE" mode then select the "HI" pressure level. Then, set timer to 2 minutes and press "STOP/START"; it will start the cooking process by building up inside pressure.

5. When the timer goes off, release pressure by adjusting the pressure valve to the VENT. After pressure gets released, open the pressure lid.

6. Add the mayonnaise mixture and stir. Seal multi-cooker by using crisping lid to lock it; ensure to keep pressure release valve locked/sealed.

7. Select "BROIL" mode and select the "HI" pressure level. Then, set timer to 5 minutes and press "STOP/START"; it will start the cooking process by building up inside pressure.

8. When the timer goes off, quickly release pressure by adjusting the pressure valve to the VENT.

9. After pressure gets released, open the Crisping Lid. Serve warm with the parsley on top.

Crisped Brussel Sprouts

Brussel sprouts are delicious when grilled and now you can enjoy them too.

Serves: 4

Time: 22 mins.

Ingredients:

- Brussels sprouts (1 pound, halved)
- olive oil (2 tablespoons, extra-virgin)
- black pepper (½ teaspoon ground)
- sea salt (1 teaspoon)
- bacon (6 slices, chopped)

Directions:

1. In a mixing bowl, toss the Brussels sprouts, olive oil, salt, black pepper, and bacon.

2. Arrange Electric grill over your kitchen platform, then open the top lid. Arrange the Crisping Basket inside the pot.

3. Press "AIR CRISP" and adjust the temperature to 390°F. Adjust the timer to 12 minutes and then press "START/STOP."

4. Electric grill will start pre-heating. Once Electric grill is fully functional and preheated it should start to beep.

5. Once you hear a beep, open top lid. Arrange the Brussels sprout mixture directly inside the basket.

6. Close the top lid and cook for 6 minutes. After 6 minutes, shake the basket and close the top lid and cook for another 6 minutes. Serve warm.

'Cajun' Eggplant Appetizer

Cajun is a powerful spice but when added to grilled eggplant, it provides the perfect balance.

Serves: 4

Time: 20 mins.

Ingredients:

- lime juice (2 tablespoons)
- Cajun seasoning (3 teaspoons)
- Eggplants (2 small, cut into slices (1/2 inch))
- olive oil (1/4 cup)

Directions:

1. Coat the eggplant slices with the oil, lemon juice, and Cajun seasoning.

2. Next arrange Electric grill, over your kitchen platform, then open the top lid. Evenly arrange the grill grate then close the top lid.

3. Press the "GRILL" function then select the "MED" grill function. Adjust timer to approx., 10 minutes then press "START/STOP" function. Electric grill should start to pre-heat.

4. Once Electric grill begins to beep, it is fully functional and preheated After you hear a beep, open the top lid.

5. Arrange the eggplant slices over the grill grate.

6. Close the top lid and cook for 5 minutes. Now open the top lid, flip the eggplant slices.

7. Close the top lid and cook for 5 more minutes. Divide into serving plates. Serve warm.

Basil Shrimp Appetizer

These shrimps make for the perfect appetizer.

Serves: 4-6

Time: 18 mins.

Ingredients:

- olive oil (2 teaspoons)
- Black pepper (ground) and salt to taste
- Shrimp (1 pound, peeled and deveined)
- Basil (1 tablespoon, chopped)

Directions:

1. Take Electric grill multi-cooker, arrange it over a cooking platform, and open the top lid.

2. In the pot, place the Crisping Basket. In the basket, add all the ingredients and combine them.

3. Seal multi-cooker by using crisping lid to lock it; ensure to keep pressure release valve locked/sealed.

4. Select the "AIR CRISP" mode and adjust the 370°F temperature level.

5. Then after, set timer to 8 minutes and press "STOP/START," it will start the cooking process by building up inside pressure.

6. When the timer goes off, quickly release pressure by adjusting the pressure valve to the VENT.

7. After pressure gets released, open the Crisping Lid. Serve warm.

Crisped Brussel Sprouts

Brussel sprouts are delicious when grilled and now you can enjoy them too.

Serves: 4

Time: 18 mins.

Ingredients:

Pineapple:

- pineapple (1)
- honey (3 tablespoons)
- lime juice (2 tablespoons)
- sugar (1/4 cup packed brown)

Dip:

- cream cheese (3 ounces, softened)
- sugar (1 tablespoon brown)
- lime juice (1 tablespoon)
- honey (2 tablespoons)
- yogurt (1/4 cup)
- lime zest (1 teaspoon grated)

Directions:

1. Firstly, make 8 wedges using the pineapple then divide each wedge into 2 spears.

2. Combine spears using the lime juice, sugar, and honey; refrigerate for approximately 1 hour.

3. Combine all dip ingredients into another bowl then set aside.

4. Remove pineapple spears from bowl then take the Electric grill, evenly arrange over kitchen platform, then open top lid.

5. Arrange the grill grate then close the top lid. Press the "GRILL" function then select the "MED" grill function.

6. Adjust timer to 8 minutes then press the "START/STOP." Electric grill should start to preheat.

7. Electric grill should start to beep once it is fully functional and preheated.

8. Once you have heard a beep, proceed to open top lid. Arrange the spears over the grill grate.

9. Close top lid then cook for approximately 4 minutes then open top lid and flip the spears.

10. Close top lid then cook for an additional 4 minutes. Divide into serving plates. Serve warm with the prepared dip.

Chicken Alfredo Apples

This dinner recipe will quickly become a family favorite.

Serves: 4

Time: 30 mins.

Ingredients:

- Apple (1 large, wedged)
- lemon juice (1 tablespoon)
- chicken breasts (4, halved)
- chicken seasoning (4 teaspoons)
- provolone cheese (4 slices)
- blue cheese (1/4 cup, crumbled)
- Alfredo sauce (1/2 cup)

Directions:

1. Use the chicken seasoning to season the chicken into a bowl. In another bowl, toss apple using lemon juice.

2. Arrange the Electric grill, over kitchen platform, then open top lid. Arrange grill grate then close top lid.

3. Press the "GRILL" then select the "MED" grill function. Adjust timer to approx.,16 minutes then press the "START/STOP" function.

4. Electric grill should start to preheat. Electric grill should begin beeping once preheated and fully functional.

5. Once you have heard a beep, open top lid then arrange chicken over grill grate. Close top lid then, cook for approx., 8 minutes.

6. Now open top lid then, flip the chicken. Close top lid then, cook for an additional 8 minutes.

7. When finished, grill apple in the same manner for approx., 2 minutes per side.

8. Serve chicken using the blue cheese, apple, and alfredo sauce.

Grilled Orange Chicken

This recipe produces a juicy, succulent, and grilled chicken.

Serves: 5-6

Time: 20 mins.

Ingredients:

- coriander (2 teaspoons ground)
- garlic salt (1/2 teaspoon)
- black pepper
- chicken wings (12)
- canola oil (1 tablespoon)
- Sauce:
- Butter (1/4 cup melted)
- honey (3 tablespoons)
- orange juice (1/2 cup)
- Sriracha chili sauce (1/3 cup)
- lime juice (2 tablespoons
- cilantro (1/4 cup chopped)

Directions:

1. Using oil and season with spices coat the chicken; refrigerate for 2 hours to marinate.

2. Merge all the sauce ingredients then set aside. Optionally, you can stir the sauce mixture for 3-4 minutes in a saucepan.

3. Place the Electric grill on your kitchen platform, then open the top lid.

4. Arrange the Electric grill grate and Seal the top lid.

5. Press "GRILL" and select the "MED" grill function. Adjust the timer to 10 minutes and then press "START/STOP." Electric grill will start pre-heating.

6. When the Electric grill starts to beep it is preheated and ready to cook. Afterwards, open the top lid.

7. Place the chicken over the grill grate.

8. Close the top lid and cook for 5 minutes. Now open the top lid, flip the chicken.

9. Close the top lid and cook for 5 more minutes. Serve warm with the prepared sauce on top.

Turkey Cream Noodles

This Turkey Cream Noodles works great as heavy lunch or dinner.

Serves: 4

Time: 45 mins.

Ingredients:

- cremini mushrooms (8 ounces, sliced)
- condensed cream of celery soup (1 10.5 oz. can)
- butter (2 tbsp.)
- ground turkey (1 lbs.)
- peas (16 oz.)
- sour cream (1 cup)
- Parmesan cheese (¾ cup, grated)
- chicken stock (¾ cup)
- package egg noodles (1,10 oz.)
- Kosher salt
- black pepper (Fresh, ground)

Directions:

1. Place the Electric grill multi-cooker on a cooking platform, then open the top lid.

2. Put butter in the pot; Select "SEAR/SAUTÉ" mode and select "MD: HI" pressure level. Press "STOP/START."

3. After approximately 5 minutes, the butter should melt.

4. Put in the mushrooms and the turkey and stir-cook for approximately 10 minutes to brown evenly.

5. Add the condensed soup and stock then stir and allow to simmer for 15 minutes.

6. Add the egg noodles and peas; stir-cook for 8-10 minutes until the noodles are cooked well done.

7. Add the sour cream and Parmesan cheese; stir the mixture. Season with salt and pepper. Serve warm.

Classic Herbed Turkey

Produce a juicy holiday turkey lunch or dinner with this simple dinner.

Serves: 4

Time: 25 mins.

Ingredients:

- Oregano (¼ tsp., dried)
- turkey breasts (1 lbs., boneless)
- garlic powder (½ tsp.)
- butter (4 tbsp., melted)
- salt (4 tbsp.)
- black pepper (1 tsp.)
- basil (¼ tsp. dried)

Directions:

1. Season the meat with the garlic powder, dried basil, dried oregano, salt, and pepper.

2. Take Electric grill multi-cooker, arrange it over a cooking platform, and open the top lid.

3. In the pot, add the butter; Select "SEAR/SAUTÉ" mode and select "MD: HI" pressure level.

4. Press "STOP/START." After about 4-5 minutes, the butter will start simmering.

5. Add the turkey breasts and stir-cook for about 2-3 minutes to brown evenly.

6. Seal multi-cooker by using crisping lid to lock it; ensure to keep pressure release valve locked/sealed.

7. Select "BAKE/ROAST" mode and adjust the 355°F temperature level.

8. Then, set timer to 15 minutes and press "STOP/START"; it will start the cooking process by building up inside pressure.

9. Serve warm and enjoy!

Turkey Bean Chili

This chili can be whipped up in minutes and delicious.

Serves: 6

Time: 40 mins.

Ingredients:

- garlic cloves (2, minced)

- turkey (1 ½ pounds, ground)

- olive oil (1 tablespoon, extra-virgin)

- onion (1, chopped)

- oregano (1 tablespoon, dried)

- cumin (1 tablespoon ground)

- cannellini beans (3 (15-ounce) cans, drained and rinsed)

- sea salt (⅛ teaspoon)

- black pepper (⅛ teaspoon, freshly ground)

- chicken broth (4 cups)

- biscuits (1 pack)

Directions:

1. Take Electric grill multi-cooker, arrange it over a cooking platform, and open the top lid.

2. In the pot, add the oil; Select "SEAR/SAUTÉ" mode and select "MD: HI" pressure level.

3. Press "STOP/START." After about 4-5 minutes, the oil will start simmering.

4. Add the onions, garlic, and cook (while stirring) for 2-3 minutes until they become softened and translucent.

5. Add the turkey, cumin, oregano, beans, broth, salt, and black pepper; stir the mixture.

6. Seal multi-cooker by using crisping lid to lock it; ensure to keep pressure release valve locked/sealed.

7. Select "PRESSURE" mode and select the "HI" pressure level. Then, set timer to 10 minutes and press "STOP/START"; it will start the cooking process by building up inside pressure.

8. Once timer has elapsed, quickly release the pressure by adjusting pressure valve to the VENT. After pressure gets released, open the pressure lid.

9. Evenly arrange biscuits into a single layer over mixture.

10. Seal multi-cooker by using crisping lid to lock it; ensure to keep pressure release valve locked/sealed.

11. Select "BROIL" mode and select the "HI" pressure level. Then, set timer to 15 minutes and press "STOP/START"; it will start the cooking process by building up inside pressure.

12. When timer goes off, quickly release pressure by adjusting pressure valve to the VENT.

13. After pressure gets released, open the pressure lid. Serve warm and enjoy!

Chicken Alfredo Pear

Adding pear to your Chicken Alfredo gives you a blast of flavor in every bite.

Serves: 4

Time: 30 mins.

Ingredients:

- Pear (1 large, wedged)
- lemon juice (1 tablespoon)
- chicken breasts (4, halved)
- chicken seasoning (4 teaspoons)
- provolone cheese (4 slices)
- blue cheese (1/4 cup, crumbled)
- Alfredo sauce (1/2 cup)

Directions:

1. Use chicken seasoning to season chicken into a bowl. In another bowl, toss apple using lemon juice.

2. Arrange Electric grill, over your kitchen platform, then open top lid. Arrange grill grate then close top lid.

3. Press the "GRILL" function then select the "MED" grill function.

4. Adjust timer for 16 minutes then press "START/STOP function Electric grill should start to preheat.

5. Once Electric grill is fully functional and preheated it should start to beep. Once you hear a beep, open the top lid.

6. Arrange the chicken over the grill grate. Close the top lid and cook for 8 minutes. Now open the top lid, flip the chicken.

7. Close the top lid and cook for 8 more minutes.

8. Then after, grill the apple in the same manner for 2 minutes per side.

9. Serve the chicken with the apple, blue cheese, and alfredo sauce.

Chicken Bean Bake

This Chicken Bean Bake is a hassle free and delicious.

Serves: 8

Time: 30 mins.

Ingredients:

- red onion (½, diced)
- red bell pepper (½, diced)
- extra-virgin olive oil (1 tbsp.)
- chicken breasts (2, 8 oz., boneless, skinless, cut into 1-inch cubes)
- rice (1 cup, white)
- corn (1, 15 oz. can, rinsed)
- Tomatoes (1, 10 oz. can, roasted with chiles)
- black beans (1, 15 oz. can, rinsed and drained)
- taco seasoning (1, 1 oz. packet)
- Cheddar cheese (2 cups, shredded)
- chicken broth (2 cups)
- Kosher salt
- Black pepper (ground)

Directions:

1. Take Electric grill multi-cooker, arrange it over a cooking platform, and open the top lid.

2. In a pot, add the oil, select "SEAR/SAUTÉ" mode and select "MD: HI" pressure level. Press "STOP/START." After about 4-5 minutes, the oil will start simmering.

3. Add the chicken and stir cook for about 2-3 minutes to brown evenly.

4. Add the onion and bell pepper, stir-cook until softened for 2 minutes.

5. Add the rice, tomatoes, beans, corn, taco seasoning, broth, salt, and pepper, combine well.

6. Seal multi-cooker by using crisping lid to lock it; ensure to keep pressure release valve locked/sealed.

7. Select "PRESSURE" mode and select the "HI" pressure level. Then after, set timer to 7 minutes and press "STOP/START," it will start the cooking process by building up inside pressure.

8. When the timer goes off, quickly release pressure by adjusting the pressure valve to the VENT. After pressure gets released, open the pressure lid. Add the cheese on top.

9. Seal multi-cooker by using crisping lid to lock it; ensure to keep pressure release valve locked/sealed.

10. Select "BROIL" mode and select the "HI" pressure level. Then after, set timer to 8 minutes and press "STOP/START," it will start the cooking process by building up inside pressure.

11. When the timer goes off, quickly release pressure by adjusting the pressure valve to the VENT.

12. After pressure gets released, open the Crisping Lid. Serve warm with sour cream or diced avocado on top (optional).

Turkey Yogurt Meal

This Turkey dinner is another meal that will be a family favorite.

Serves: 4

Time: 30 mins.

Ingredients:

- yogurt (14 ounces)
- ginger (1 tablespoon, grated)
- turkey breasts (2, skinless, boneless and cubed)
- onion (1 yellow, chopped)
- turmeric powder (1 teaspoon)
- olive oil (2 teaspoons)
- Black pepper (ground, salt to taste)

Directions:

1. Take Electric grill multi-cooker, arrange it over a cooking platform, and open the top lid.

2. In the pot, add the oil, select "SEAR/SAUTÉ" mode and select "MD: HI" pressure level. Press "STOP/START."

3. After about 4-5 minutes, the oil will start simmering. Add the onions and cook (while stirring) until they become softened and translucent for 4 minutes.

4. Add the ginger and turmeric, stir-cook for 1 more minute. Add remaining ingredients, stir gently.

5. Seal multi-cooker by using crisping lid to lock it; ensure to keep pressure release valve locked/sealed.

6. Select "PRESSURE" mode and select the "HI" pressure level. Then after, set timer to 20 minutes and press "STOP/START," it will start the cooking process by building up inside pressure.

7. When the timer goes off, naturally release inside pressure for about 8-10 minutes.

8. Then, quick-release pressure by adjusting the pressure valve to the VENT. Serve warm.

Exotic Pilaf Chicken

Adding grilled chicken to your Pilaf to give it a rich smoky flavor.

Serves: 4

Time: 25 mins.

Ingredients:

- butter (1 tbsp., unsalted)
- chicken thighs (4, boneless, skin-on)
- rice pilaf (1, 6-ounce box)
- water (1 ¾ cups)
- extra-virgin olive oil (1 tbsp.)
- garlic powder (1 tsp)
- kosher salt (1 tsp)

Directions:

1. Place the Electric grill multi-cooker over a cooking platform, then open the top lid.

2. In the pot, add water, butter, and pilaf, then insert a reversible rack in the pot. Put the chicken thighs over the rack.

3. Seal multi-cooker by using crisping lid to lock it; ensure to keep pressure release valve locked/sealed.

4. Select "PRESSURE" mode and select the "HI" pressure level. Then after, set timer to 4 minutes and press "STOP/START," it will start the cooking process by building up inside pressure.

5. When the timer goes off, quickly release pressure by adjusting the pressure valve to the VENT. After pressure gets released, open the pressure lid.

6. In a mixing bowl, combine together the olive oil, salt, and garlic powder. Brush thickens with this mixture.

7. Seal multi-cooker by using crisping lid to lock it; ensure to keep pressure release valve locked/sealed.

8. Select "BROIL" mode and select the "HI" pressure level. Then after, set timer to 10 minutes and press "STOP/START," it will start the cooking process by building up inside pressure.

9. When the timer goes off, quickly release pressure by adjusting the pressure valve to the VENT.

10. After pressure gets released, open the Crisping Lid. Serve warm the chicken with cooked pilaf.

Grilled BBQ Turkey

Now you can make a delicious barbecue right from your grill.

Serves: 5-6

Time: 40 mins.

Ingredients:

- Parsley (1/2 cup minced)
- onions (1/2 cup chopped green)
- garlic cloves (4, minced)
- Greek yogurt (1 cup)
- lemon juice (1/2 cup)
- rosemary (1 teaspoon dried, crushed)
- canola oil (1/3 cup)
- dill (4 tablespoons minced)
- salt (1 teaspoon)
- pepper (1/2 teaspoon)
- turkey breast (1 3-pound, half, bone in)

Directions:

1. Add all ingredients into a mixing bowl then combine, except turkey.

2. Add and coat the turkey evenly. Refrigerate for 8 hours to marinate.

3. Arrange Electric grill over your kitchen platform, then open top lid.

4. Arrange grill grate then close the top lid. Afterwards press "GRILL" then select "HIGH" setting.

5. Adjust the timer to 30 minutes then press "START/STOP." Afterwards the Electric grill will start pre-heating.

6. Once Electric grill is fully functional and preheated it should start to beep.

7. Once you have heard a beep, open top lid. Arrange turkey evenly over grill grate.

8. Close the top lid and cook for 15 minutes. Now open the top lid, flip the turkey.

9. Close the top lid and cook for 15 more minutes. Cook until the food thermometer reaches 350°F. Slice and serve.

Chicken Hot BBQ

These tasty chicken wings can be whipped up from your electrical grill.

Serves: 4

Time: 28 mins.

Ingredients:

- Honey (2 tbsp)
- chicken drumsticks (1 lbs.)
- hot sauce (1 tbsp.)
- barbecue sauce (2 cups)
- Juice of lime (1)
- Ground black pepper and sea salt (to taste)

Directions:

1. Using a mixing bowl, place the barbecue sauce, lime juice, honey, pepper, salt, and hot sauce. mix and set aside.

2. Using a mixing bowl, add the ½ cup of the sauce and chicken. Combine the ingredients to mix well with each other.

3. Refrigerate for 1 hour to marinate. Place the Electric grill over your kitchen platform, open the top lid.

4. Set up the grill grate and seal the top lid. Afterwards Press the "GRILL" setting and select the "MED" grill setting.

5. Change the timer to 18 minutes then press "START/STOP." Electric grill will start pre-heating.

6. When it starts to beep Electric grill is preheated and ready to cook. Afterwards, open the top lid. Place the chicken over the grill grate.

7. Close the top lid and allow to cook until the timer reads zero. Cook until the food thermometer reaches 165°F. Serve warm.

Moroccan Roasted Chicken

This tasty chicken dish is great for family dinner.

Serves: 4

Time: 32 mins.

Ingredients:

- yogurt (3 tbsp., plain)
- chicken thighs (4, skinless, boneless)
- garlic cloves (4, chopped)
- Kosher salt (½ tsp.)
- olive oil (1/3 cup)
- parsley (1/2 cup, fresh flat leaf, finely chopped)
- cumin (2 tsp., ground)
- paprika (2 tsp.)
- red pepper flakes (1/4 tsp., crushed)

Directions:

1. Take food processor or blender, open the lid and inside add the garlic, yogurt, salt, and oil.

2. Blend to make a smooth mixture. Refrigerate the mixture.

3. In a mixing bowl, add the chicken, red pepper flakes, paprika, cumin, parsley, and garlic. Combine the ingredients to mix well with each other. Refrigerate for 2-4 hours to marinate.

4. Place the Electric grill over your kitchen platform, then open the top lid. Grease the cooking pot lightly with some oil or cooking spray.

5. Press "ROAST" setting then adjust the temperature to 400°F. Afterwards Adjust the timer to 23 minutes and then press "START/STOP." Electric grill will begin pre-heating.

6. When it starts to beep Electric grill is preheated and ready to cook. After you hear a beep, open the top lid.

7. Place the chicken directly inside the pot.

8. Seal the top lid and cook for about 15 minutes. Now open the top lid, flip the chicken.

9. Close the top lid and cook for 8 more minutes. Serve warm with the yogurt dip.

Conclusion

You have done it! Thanks for going all the way to the end with us! I hope the delicious recipes presented in this book were enjoyed by you, and you were enlightened as to what proper grilling entails and the superb recipes that you can prepare on it.

Continue to practice and do your own creation by mixing and matching the tasty recipes we have presented to you, then share with your family and friends!

Cheers!

Author's Afterthoughts

thank you

I can't find the perfect words to tell you how grateful I am that you gave this book a chance. I know it must not have been easy seeking this book out and going for it, especially since there are multitudes of materials out there with related content.

You bought the book, but you didn't stop there. You continued, took this journey with me, and read every page back to back. I have to say, you make all this worth it.

I would like to know your thoughts about this book too. Your comments may also help others who are yet to download this book make a decision. What's better than one person reading a book? Two people reading it.

For my new books, follow my author page at http://www.graceberry.net

Thank you,

Grace Berry

About the Author

Grace Berry started as a book reviewer after she graduated from college with a degree in creative writing. Afterward, she worked as an editor for a local magazine. She resigned her post and opted to work as a freelance journalist, writing for newspapers and magazines, online and offline.

On one of such assignments, she wrote content for a food blog – a gig she found interesting. Excited about her discovery, she delved deeper into the food world, rediscovering her concept of food. She took a break from freelancing and sought local restaurateurs and chefs out to gather everything she could about their processes and cooking methods; an encounter she documented and wrote about later.

Grace figured out that she could combine her flair for writing with her newfound love for everything food, so she took a plunge and started writing about recipes and other information related to getting the best from the kitchen to the dining.

Now, she has compiled some of her years of research and experiment into a single volume of work, combining storytelling with factual information. Grace hopes to do more, and maybe start a catering business or a restaurant of her own in the future. At the moment, though, recipe developer and cookbook writer will have to do.

Printed in Poland
by Amazon Fulfillment
Poland Sp. z o.o., Wrocław